ROMAN SHIP
MODEL

Tim Dowley   Peter Pohle

Contents

CANDLE
BOOKS

The first boats

Thousands of years before sailors first took their ships onto the open seas, men and women were sailing small vessels on the major rivers of Bible lands. They navigated the long river Nile in Egypt and the great rivers Tigris and Euphrates in Mesopotamia. The first "boats" were probably just bundles of reeds or bound-up logs that people paddled across a river or lake.

Inflated skins

An illustration on stone from ancient Assyria shows soldiers crossing a river by floating on animal skins that have been inflated. Even today, Iraqi herdsmen cross streams on similar inflated goatskins.

In time, people wanted something better than just a float so that they could travel further and more safely. Where reeds or trees were readily available, sailors tied them together to create a raft big enough to navigate a river.

Rafts

But on fast-flowing waters that passed over stony rapids, a raft would soon get broken up. So to travel on the Tigris and Euphrates, sailors started to tie together a number of

This stone was used as a ship's anchor in Bible times.

Boat with horse-head shaped prow carrying logs. From the palace of King Sargon II 721–705 BC.

inflated skins and cover them with reed matting to make a raft. Such a vessel would be big and strong enough to carry not just people but also goods and animals. When the raft passed over rapids, one or two bladders (inflated skins) might burst, but the rest would carry the raft safely on its journey, floating down the river.

Once the voyagers arrived at their destination they would unload their goods. Then they let out the air from the skins, dried them, loaded them on a donkey or camel and took them back home to use all over again.

The Greek historian Herodotus wrote about seeing such rafts in use in Babylon:

"Each raft has on board a live donkey – the larger rafts have several donkeys. After they arrive in Babylon, the men get rid of their cargo and sell the wooden frame of their raft. Next they let the air out of the skins, load them on the donkeys and walk back to Armenia, where they originally came from."

On rivers that had no hazardous rapids to cross, a raft could be supported on floats made from clay pots. These were cheaper than inflatable animal skins.

But boats didn't develop much further in Mesopotamia because the northern parts of the rivers Tigris and Euphrates are too shallow and rocky. In addition, both rivers flow southwards and the winds are also mainly from the north. For this reason it was impossible to sail upstream until the steamship was invented. Instead, boats had laboriously to be towed or carried northwards.

Boats with oars

People sailing on a raft could get very wet. And, as we have seen, it is almost impossible to sail a raft upstream against the current. So the next step was to make actual boats.

Some of the first boats were probably made of animal skins stretched over a frame made of branches. Boats were also made of reeds or papyrus, covered with skins and smeared with bitumen (tar) to make them water-tight. These boats were usually powered by short, wide oars.

Such boats came in many sizes. One-man boats of this kind were light enough to be carried on a person's back on land.

Model of an early Egyptian rowing boat.

By contrast, large skin-covered boats could hold several tons of cargo as well as a crew of sailors. Such boats – called "coracles" – were widely used in ancient Mesopotamia. Archaeologists have discovered models of boats like this in a royal cemetery at Ur, Mesopotamia, dating from around 3000 BC. In ancient Egypt people used "pot boats" – floating clay containers big enough to carry at least one passenger.

Egyptian boats

The river Nile became very important in the history of water transport. This great river has 500 miles of water that can be navigated, stretching from Aswan in the south to the Nile Delta.

Egyptian tomb model of a Nile river craft, with small sail and large steering paddle.

yard

stay

boom

steering paddle

Because there were few trees in the area, the first boats were usually made of reeds or bulrushes. Starting with basic rafts built from bundles of reeds, the Egyptians gradually learned how to shape their craft into long, narrow boats. They also discovered how to make wooden paddles to propel their boats, and fixed a rudder towards the back of their boats to steer them.

A heavily loaded Nile boat, powered by an oar.

These little boats were fine for sailing the peaceful river Nile – but much too flimsy for the stormy Mediterranean.

The first sails

In Egypt, sailors first started to make boats with sails. They began by fixing a tall, leafy palm branch upright at the front of the boat. When the wind blew, it caught the fronds of the branch and helped move the boat along.

From about 3500 BC the Egyptians began to use more normal sails. They probably made these out of leaves or branches. They wove the branches into a square shape and hung the sail from a pole (yard) fixed to the top of a vertical wooden mast fixed towards the front (forward) of the boat. These first Nile sailing boats were very light and didn't have a keel (a board sticking out beneath a boat that helps keep it stable).

The mast on these early Egyptian sailing boats was supported by ropes (stays) fastened to its top and tied to the front, back and sides of the vessel. In time, shipbuilders moved the

mast's position back until it was normally placed in the middle of the ship (amidships).

In addition to the yard, the sail often had a second pole (boom) fastened to its bottom edge. Later, sails were made of papyrus, or linen on bigger ships, instead of leaves. We have a good idea of what these Egyptian vessels looked like as the pharaohs often had ship models buried with them. Archaeologists have unearthed many of these models. Some have a number of rowers or paddlers, while others carry the coffin of a pharaoh. Archaeologists have even discovered a full-

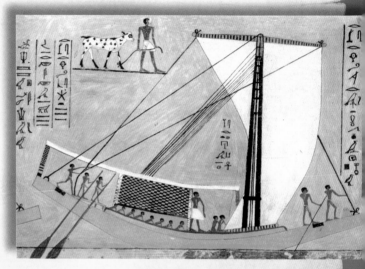

A Nile sailing boat with its crew, from the tomb of Pharaoh Thutmose IV 1420-11 BC.

size Egyptian boat dating from around 2500 BC near the great Pyramid of Cheops at Giza, Egypt.

Wooden boats

Although these reed boats were fine for gliding across the Nile, they couldn't carry heavy loads. As we know from the pyramids, the Egyptians were great monument builders and needed to transport heavy building stones. Possibly for this reason they began to build boats from wood. At first, they made the new wooden boats in the same shape as the old reed boats.

The main wood available in Egypt came from the acacia tree. However, acacia is brittle

5

and comes in short lengths. For this reason, it's not very good for boat-building. The Egyptian carpenters discovered that by fixing together short planks of acacia wood they could build up the hull (body) of a ship.

Even these wooden ships weren't very strong, though they were good enough to sail on a river. On bigger boats the carpenters often added a wooden floor (deck) that helped strengthen the boat. On some boats they also built a little shelter or cabin on the deck, made up of a wooden frame covered with mats.

Some Egyptian Nile vessels were huge. Queen Hatshepsut, who reigned round 1500 BC, built barges that could carry huge stone obelisks (four-sided tapering columns, like Cleopatra's Needle in London) nearly 30 metres (100 feet) high

A Philistine warrior.

from Aswan to Karnak, a distance of about 200 kilometres (125 miles).

Bigger ships

In time, the Egyptians built larger, stronger boats that could go to sea. They began to travel to many places on the Red Sea and Mediterranean Sea, buying and selling goods. Queen Hatshepsut sent sea-going ships down the Red Sea to a place the Egyptians called "Punt" – probably the coast of modern Somalia or Ethiopia.

From as early as 2300 BC ships were also used in warfare – to transport soldiers and as fighting vessels. For military use, the galley was particularly valued. Galleys were long, thin vessels, powered by one or more lines of rowers on each side. Wider versions were also used for transporting goods. Since this book mainly concerns the Roman merchant ship, we will not discuss in detail the growth of naval warfare.

By 1400 BC sea-going merchant ships had certainly appeared. A wall-painting from Thebes, Egypt, shows a fleet of such trading vessels entering port. The ships are broad – not narrow like oared galleys – and have no oarsmen. Some are shown being unloaded by sailors. The fleet pictured – which was not Egyptian – probably came from the eastern Mediterranean.

The Sea People

Around 1200 BC a new sea-going people arrived in the eastern Mediterranean. The "Sea People", a war-like and sea-faring nation, sailed east from Aegean islands in the western Mediterranean at this time.

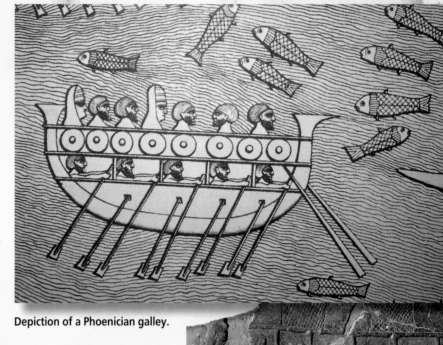

Depiction of a Phoenician galley.

Assyrian depiction of a Phoenician galley. Notice the pointed prow.

The Sea People brought with them new skills in building and navigating ships. For instance, they no longer fitted a boom at the bottom of the sail. This allowed them to use a system of ropes (lines) to furl and unfurl the sail during a voyage. By doing this, they could prevent strong winds from damaging the ship when the sails were unfurled.

Part of the Sea People, the Philistines, tried to invade Egypt but were beaten back by the Egyptian ruler Ramesses III in a great sea-battle at the mouth of the Nile. Egyptian artists pictured the battle on a wall-carving at Medinet Habu, near Thebes. The Philistine ships were very shallow, with one mast and

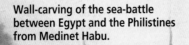

Wall-carving of the sea-battle between Egypt and the Philistines from Medinet Habu.

no rudder. They had a raised prow and stern (front and back) to protect sailors from the waves.

Beaten back by the Egyptians, the Philistines settled on the coast of Israel and became fierce enemies of the Israelites.

The Phoenician master-mariners

The Phoenicians also inhabited a strip of the Mediterranean coast of Israel, north of the Philistines. From about 1100 BC, the Phoenicians, with the Greeks, took over from the Egyptians as the great sailors of the Mediterranean region. They used fine timber from the great cedar forests of Lebanon to build their ships.

The Phoenicians soon became known as the best navigators of ancient times. Their city of Byblos (north

Port of Eilat (ancient Elath).

of modern Beirut) became an important Mediterranean trading port. Ships from Byblos carried cedar wood from Lebanon to Egypt and returned loaded with papyrus and farm products – grain and fruit – that they then took to other places in the Mediterranean to sell.

Galilee fisherman.

Phoenician ships

At first, the Phoenicians had only small ships powered with oars, so they kept to the shallow waters near the coast. But once they started to put sails on their boats, they began to venture further. Soon the Phoenicians were making long voyages as far as the west coast of Spain, north Africa and even southern England.

We do not have any Phoenician drawings of their ships. However, the Assyrians drew some Phoenician ships on stone tablets (see central picture). These Assyrian pictures show that Phoenician boats

Model of a Philistine sailing boat, 10th–8th century BC. Notice the two big oars for steering.

were usually tall, with just one high mast. They were quite broad boats, and rounded at both ends. The Phoenician vessels were often decorated on the prow (projecting front part) with a horse's head – the Greeks nicknamed them "horses". Phoenician ships were often powered with both sails and oars. In the Mediterranean, they usually sailed north, blown by the wind in their sails; and back south – against the wind – powered by their oars.

Mending nets at Acre (ancient Akko).

The Greeks take over

The Assyrians were very warlike, and after about 750 BC their armies prevented the Phoenicians from sailing and trading so widely. The Greeks now began to take over from the Phoenicians, sailing to more and more places across the Mediterranean and trading with many different nations. By the time of their great leader, Alexander the Great (356-323 BC), Greek sailors setting out from the Red Sea had reached as far south as the west coast of India.

Artist's impression of two fishing boats of Bible times on the Sea of Galilee.

Ships in the Bible

You won't find ships mentioned much in the Old Testament. The Jews were mainly farmers and didn't feel too comfortable with the sea. Between their land and the Mediterranean Sea there lived for many years the warlike Phoenicians and Philistines.

Some of the Jews seem to have been quite frightened of the sea and the wild monsters they thought lived there. During the reign of King David, Israel began to trade quite actively with the kingdom of Tyre. This led to the Israelites' building more ships and sailing

Ancient fishing boat discovered near Kibbutz Ginnosar, Galilee.

more widely. David's son, King Solomon, founded a merchant fleet at Ezion-Geber (1 Kings 9:26), on the Red Sea, to trade with Ophir (probably Punt, in Africa), and possibly even as far as southern India (1 Kings 10:22).

"King Solomon also built ships at Ezion Geber, which is near Elath in Edom, on the shore of the Red Sea. And Hiram [of Tyre] sent his men – sailors who knew the sea – to serve in the fleet with Solomon's men. They sailed to Ophir and brought back 420 talents of gold, which they delivered to King Solomon."
(1 Kings 9:26–28, NIV)

However Solomon's navy was made up of Phoenician ships and manned largely with Phoenician sailors (2 Chronicles 9:21). After this time, the Bible makes little mention of Israelite ships. One exception is the prophet Ezekiel when he says God is unhappy with the people of Tyre. He describes in detail a ship of Tyre, with its inlaid ivory and embroidered purple sails:

"You were like a great ship built of the finest cypress from Hermon. They took a cedar from Lebanon to make a mast for you. They carved oars for you from the oaks of Bashan. They made your deck of pine wood, brought from the southern coasts of Cyprus. Then they inlaid it with ivory. Your sails were made of Egypt's finest linen, and they flew as a banner above you. You stood beneath the blue and purple awnings made bright with dyes from the coasts of Elishah.

"Your oarsmen came from Sidon and Arvad; your helmsmen were skilled men from Tyre itself. Wise old craftsmen from Gebal did all the caulking. Ships came with goods from every land to barter for your trade."
(Ezekiel 27:5–9, NLT)

The shipbuilding materials that Ezekiel lists were the best available in the eastern Mediterranean. The Egyptians preferred pine and fir for their ships' masts and yards. The oars were made of hardwood, for strength. And the dyes used to colour the awnings were the most expensive available. Caulking was the job of making the ship's

seams (gaps between the planks) watertight, often by pressing tarred rope into them.

New Testament

Fishing

Fishing and fishing-boats are often mentioned in the Gospels. Four of the disciples, Jesus' closest followers, were fishermen – Peter and Andrew, James and John. They all fished on the Sea of Galilee.

The boats of the Sea of Galilee that we read about in the Gospels, and that Jesus knew, were sturdy fishing vessels that could comfortably hold at least twelve people (Luke 5:7).

A Galilee boat

In January 1986 an ancient boat was discovered buried in mud on the north shore of the Sea of Galilee, near Kibbutz Ginnosar.

Mosaic of a Roman ship discovered at Lod, Israel.

Archaeologists used scientific tests, called Carbon 14 tests, to try to find out how old the boat was. They managed to date it to between the first century BC and the end of the first century AD – roughly the time of Jesus.

Archaeologists carefully dug out the buried boat. They discovered that it measured 8 metres (26.5 feet) long,

2.3 metres (7.5 feet) wide and 1.3 metres (4.5 feet) high. It was the first ancient fishing boat found on an inland lake in the Mediterranean area.

The archaeologists were keen to preserve their unique discovery. They strengthened the fragile wooden boat by building frames made of fibreglass and polyester resin to form a protective shell around it. They then transported the boat the short distance to a museum at Ginnosar. There archaeologists treated it with special chemicals to ensure it is preserved for the future.

The Galilee boat had a single mast for sailing, as well as two oars on each side. It would have carried up to fifteen men, so Jesus and his disciples could easily have fitted into such a boat. Jesus was probably sleeping in the stern (back part) of a boat like this when the storm blew up on the Sea of Galilee (Mark 4:37–41).

Roman Ships

Before the Romans

From earliest times there were no new great leaps forward in shipbuilding methods until the Romans. However the Romans made great improvements in all areas of shipping.

Ancient ships were usually made of wood and constructed with a keel, ribs and planking caulked with tar. Both ends of the keel – fore and aft (front and back) – normally extended well above the level of the deck and were decorated with figureheads.

Before 400 BC, merchant ships usually had a deck at least fore and aft, with an awning or cloth covering over the stern (rear) deck (see Ezekiel 27:7). After that time most merchant ships had a deck right across their length and breadth.

Such ships were usually less than 30 metres (100 feet) long.

Until Roman times, most ships had a single mast with a square sail. Later ships often also had a foremast and foresail (a mast slanting forwards from the bows, with a sail fastened to it).

Ancient Mediterranean ships had only a side rudder, a huge oar fitted in a slanting position near the stern. The steersman pushed or pulled a tiller bar to vary the angle of this oar and so steer the ship. On later boats, the steering mechanism more often

Sculpture of a Roman river-going merchant vessel carrying barrels.

consisted of two oars, one on each side of the boat's stern.

Roman merchant ships

In Roman times there were two main types of ship: long, narrow, fast vessels used mainly in war; and wide, heavy vessels used to carry goods and passengers. The long ships (Latin: *naves longae*) included triremes (with three banks of oars and three rows of oarsmen) and quinqueremes (with five banks of oars and five rows of oarsmen).

Roman merchant ships were designed to stay at sea for long periods in most weathers, and to carry heavy and bulky goods.

Artist's impression of a Roman merchant ship under sail. Notice the galley in the background.

9

Roman Ship Model

Sternpost in shape of swan's neck and head

Deckhouse with cabins for officers and important passengers

Long rudder on each side (port and starboard)

Artist's impression of fishing and mending nets on the Sea of Galilee.

Shrouds

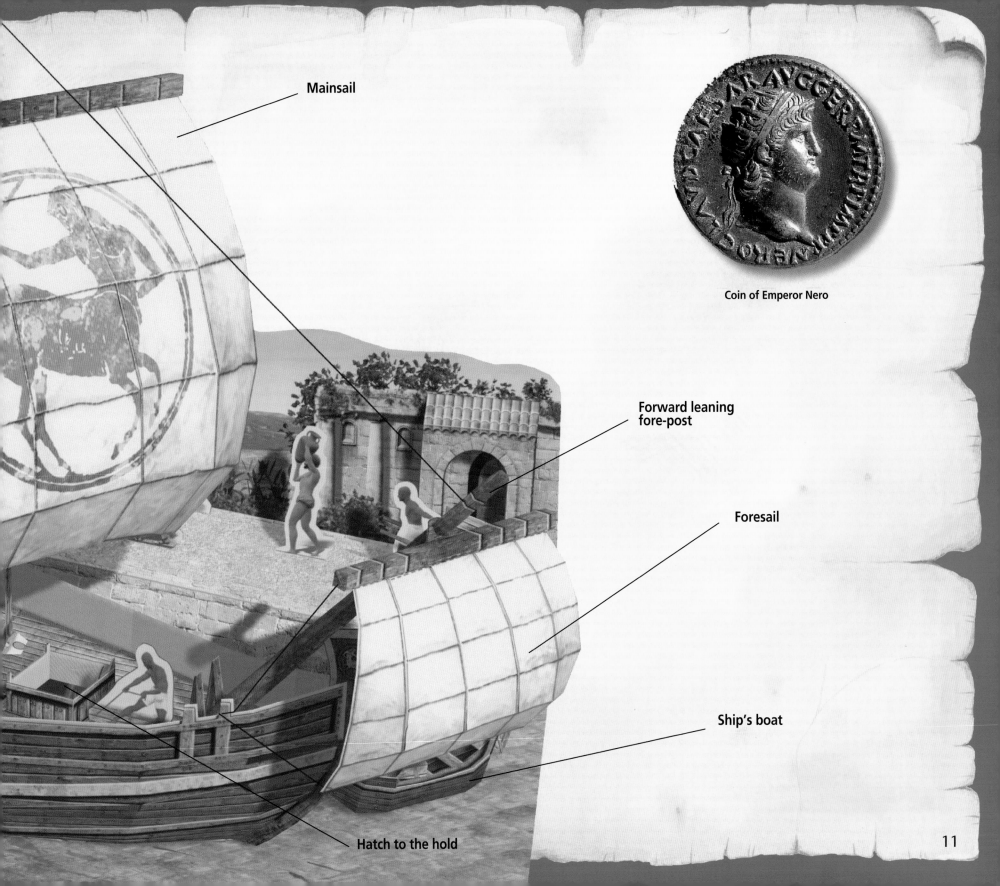

Mainsail

Forward leaning
fore-post

Foresail

Ship's boat

Hatch to the hold

Coin of Emperor Nero

11

The Romans built their merchant ships mainly from wood, with a simple prow (projecting front part). They raised the aft (back part) higher, and had the deck slope down towards the middle of the vessel. Roman shipbuilders covered the decks with wooden planks and often built one or more little wooden cabins on the decks. Behind the aft (back) cabin rose the back wooden post (sternpost), which often ended in the shape of a goose's head (Latin: *cheniscus*).

Roman merchant ships had fixed masts. Roman mariners used mainly sails at sea, although sometimes in an emergency and for additional power they also used long oars. Most merchant ships had two masts: the main central mast carrying the mainsail, and a foremast supporting a foresail.

Building Roman boats

Greek and Roman shipbuilders used pine, fir or cedar wood for the planks needed to build the hull of their ships. The Romans introduced a new form of carpentry for building ships. They locked a shell of planks together with mortised joints and strengthened the hull with a frame built inside it. They also smeared the seams of the boat – and sometimes the entire hull – with pitch, or pitch and wax, to make a protective, watertight coating. Roman shipbuilders often also covered the underwater part of the hull with lead sheets, and sandwiched a layer of tarred fabric between the hull and the lead sheeting.

The helmsman, who steered the boat, would stand between the aft deckhouse and the stern. He controlled the direction of the ship by means of two tiller bars, each connected to one of the great steering oars or rudders.

For the ship's interior, Roman shipwrights used almost any wood, though they preferred fir for the oars because it was light in weight.

The Romans usually made their ships' sails from linen, and ropes from flax, hemp, papyrus or even leather. The Romans painted their ships bright purple, blue, white, yellow or green. But pirate or reconnaissance (spy) ships were camouflaged to match the colours of the sea.

Anchors

Big merchant ships would have many large anchors, usually with a lead shaft (stock) and wooden arms and shank. Some were made of iron.

We know from Luke's story of Paul's shipwreck that anchors were carried at the front and back (bows and stern) of merchant ships. Divers have recovered hundreds of pieces of ancient anchors from the Mediterranean. One, found off the island of Malta, was nearly 4.2 metres (14 feet) long and weighed more than 1850 kg (4,000 pounds).

How big were Roman merchant ships?

The Romans built their trading boats quite wide. Some were only four times as long as they were broad. Roman merchant vessels could be very large. Some were as long as 42.5 metres (140 feet), 11 metres (36 feet) wide and 10 metres (33 feet) deep.

In Roman times the average merchant vessel probably held between 50 and 100 tons. But during the first century AD, Roman ships carrying government materials frequently carried cargoes weighing as much as 340 tons.

The biggest vessels of all belonged to the Roman imperial grain fleet. These boats could hold up to 1,200 tons and were sometimes nearly 60 metres (200 feet) long. The Alexandrian grain-ship Isis, dating to the second century AD, measured 42.5 metres (140 feet) long by 11 metres (36 feet) wide and carried cargo of up to 3250 tons.

These huge Roman merchant ships were not fast. A freighter doing a good speed averaged four to six knots, with a fair wind in the sails. (A knot is the unit of speed at sea. One knot is the equivalent of one nautical mile [about 1,853 metres or 6,080 feet] per hour.) At that speed, a ship would take about eight days to sail from Alexandria in Egypt to Puteoli in Italy. With a good wind, the journey of the apostle Paul and his friend Barnabas from Seleucia, the port of Antioch in Syria, to Salamis, on the island of Cyprus, would have taken about 24 hours (Acts 13:4–5).

If the wind was not in the right direction for the sails to catch it, the captain would take a zigzag course to make the best of the wind. This procedure, known as "tacking", was quite tricky.

When the captain needed to have his ship rowed, he either gave the oarsmen regular

Two ancient wine jars, or amphoras. Such jars would have been loaded on Roman merchant ships to transport wine and olive oil. The long pointed shaft would be slotted into a vertical hole in the deck to prevent the jar shifting at sea.

Artist's impression of Jesus calling the fishermen Peter and Andrew to follow him. Notice the typical Galilee fishing boats.

Basalt columns from the Herodian port at Caesarea.

rest periods or rotated them in squads. Rowing a large ship was very hard work – especially on a hot summer day!

Roman cargoes

Roman merchant ships carried an astonishing variety of goods from Syria, Cyprus and many other places to ports in the western Mediterranean. They sometimes delivered luxury goods that came from the Far East.

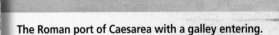

The Roman port of Caesarea with a galley entering.

(The "silk road" from China ended in Syria, just across the sea from Cyprus.)

Merchant ships carried dyes and finished goods from Syria in large quantities. They also loaded up with copper, iron, olive oil, wines and other products to take from Cyprus to markets in Asia Minor and Italy.

Amphoras

Wine, olive oil and other liquids were stored and transported in a special type of tall, thin, two-handled clay pot known as an "amphora". Sometimes these amphoras had a pointed tip to fit in a hole in the ship's timber or to stack securely onto the rows of amphoras underneath.

Fruit and olives awaiting transport by boat.

14

supplied one-third of the grain needed to feed the people of Rome.

A fleet of Roman merchant vessels carrying grain from Alexandria in Egypt would first sail north and then west. The journey took between fifty days and two months – sometimes even three months – although the return voyage to Egypt could take as little as nine days. Scholars estimate that these ships carried a total of about 135,000 tons of Egyptian grain to Italy every year.

Crew

A Roman merchant ship was usually controlled by its owner. He would pay a captain to command his vessel and its crew. Once a vessel was under way, it was usually overseen by the sailing master.

On board larger merchant vessels there was usually also a quartermaster, who supplied the crew with food and drink. Other crew members included carpenters, guards, rowers to man the ship's boats and other sailors. Sailors generally wore little or no clothing on board ship, and a tunic but no shoes or sandals when ashore.

Passengers

There were no passenger ships in ancient times. However, most merchant ships could carry between 20 and 30 passengers. Someone wanting to travel would go to the port and look for a ship that was leaving

Illustration of a smaller Roman merchant ship, cut away to show the cargo holds.

In 1967 divers discovered the wreck of a small merchant ship off Kyrenia in northern Cyprus. On board, they found 400 amphoras. Archaeologists believe the vessel sank around 300 BC. A full-scale replica of this boat was built and is now on display at Piraeus, the port of Athens, Greece.

Grain

The most important cargo in the Mediterranean in Roman times was grain from Egypt. In the time of the apostle Paul, Egypt

Artist's impression of Julius, the Roman captain, and a Jewish civilian.

for the destination he or she wanted. A Greek author wrote: "I went down to the great harbour and . . . asked about vessels sailing for Athens."

For those journeying between Rome and the Near East, the best ships were the huge grain-carrying vessels. These ships had more space on board, were safer and made the quickest journey. The Roman Emperor Caligula advised King Herod Agrippa (who heard the apostle Paul defend himself in court in Caesarea): "take a direct sailing to Alexandria. The ships are crack sailing craft and their captains are the most experienced: they drive their vessels like racehorses . . ."

Voyagers lived in a very crowded space on board ship. For example, the apostle Paul was shipwrecked on a vessel that carried as many as 276 people (Acts 27:37). The Jewish writer Josephus said he once sailed to Rome on a ship that had 600 people on board! The Roman poet Horace said that a man who sailed the high seas in such a ship needed to have oak and bronze around his heart.

Trading ships usually had a deck cabin aft (at the back) for the captain and the ship's owner to sleep in. Passengers such as Paul and his companions would have lived and slept on deck. If they wanted some privacy, they might set up a tent. No food was provided for passengers: they had to bring and prepare their own. All the ship's captain provided was space on deck and drinking water.

If the ship ran into danger, there were no lifeboats or lifebelts to save passengers. They simply had to cling to bits of wreckage. A Roman merchant ship would usually tow behind it a small boat for emergency use (see Acts 27:30).

Despite all this, sea travel was often preferred as the safest, cheapest and most comfortable means of transport!

Navigating and seamanship

Ancient navigators had no compass or sextant to tell them where they were at sea. So sailors couldn't discover the position and course of their ship very accurately. Early sailors often used the North Star (or Pole Star) to guide them.

The Phoenicians knew how to navigate using the stars as a guide (celestial

Replica of a small Galilee sailing boat of Bible times.

navigation), so they could keep sailing at night. But even so, they often stopped their vessels overnight in a port or on a beach.

For safety, ancient ships usually sailed

The Ancient Ships of Pisa

In 1998, builders in Pisa made an amazing discovery: the remains of an ancient Etruscan and Roman port –and in it several ancient ships, perfectly preserved. There were at least 16 ancient ships, 9 of which are being recovered. There are no other examples of ancient ships (1st century BC – 4th century AD) so well preserved. Perhaps even more important, the ships' cargo was found, including the most perishable things such as ropes, rigging, fishing equipment, anchors made from stone, wood and iron, baskets and fishing pots.

The port of Acre (Akko) on the Mediterranean coast of Israel.

Paul's Voyage to Rome

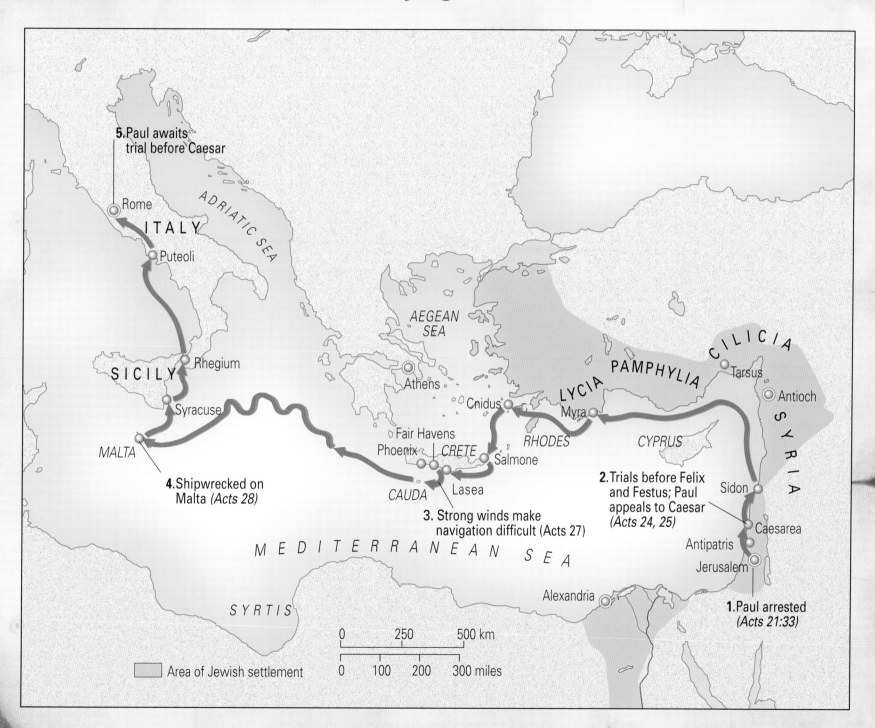

5. Paul awaits trial before Caesar

Rome

ITALY

ADRIATIC SEA

Puteoli

Rhegium

SICILY

Syracuse

MALTA

4. Shipwrecked on Malta *(Acts 28)*

SYRTIS

AEGEAN SEA

Athens

Cnidus

Fair Havens

Phoenix   *CRETE*

Lasea   Salmone

CAUDA

3. Strong winds make navigation difficult (Acts 27)

M E D I T E R R A N E A N   S E A

RHODES

CYPRUS

LYCIA   PAMPHYLIA   CILICIA

Myra   Tarsus

Antioch

SYRIA

Sidon

Caesarea

Antipatris

Jerusalem

2. Trials before Felix and Festus; Paul appeals to Caesar *(Acts 24, 25)*

1. Paul arrested *(Acts 21:33)*

Alexandria

0   250   500 km

0   100   200   300 miles

Area of Jewish settlement

hugging the coastline or hopped from one of the many Mediterranean islands to another. In an emergency, they looked for shelter behind a headland – a little ridge of land.

Many Roman ships had a little enclosure near the top of the mast, called the "crow's nest". A look-out would climb the mast and watch from the crow's nest. It allowed him to see much further than those standing on deck. The look-out would shout a warning if he saw land – or an enemy ship.

Roman sailors had a few aids to navigation. They often had handbooks with notes about the distances at sea, landmarks to watch for and ports and anchorages that were available. They also had sea-charts to help them plot their ship's course.

Sometimes the captain needed to know

Roman coin with depiction of a sailing vessel.

how deep the sea was. He would take a "sounding" to test the depth of the water. He lowered into the water a sounding pole or a line with a weight on the end to measure how deep the sea was (see Acts 27:28).

The ship's captain would use semaphore flags and lights to signal to other vessels or to land.

Sea traffic

The Romans eventually conquered most of the lands around the Mediterranean. They used their army and navy to bring peace and order to the Mediterranean world. Travel became quite safe throughout the Roman Empire.

The Roman navy ruled the Mediterranean and kept peace at sea. This helped shipping to increase and soon there were many more trading voyages carrying much larger cargoes. When the Romans built even larger ships, voyages to places as far away as India became safer and more frequent.

With larger ships, sea travel was possible at times of the year other than summer. And instead of following the coastline, merchant ships could now sail direct – for example from Alexandria to Italy with cargoes of grain. This helps explain how the apostle Paul was able to sail easily between different parts of the Roman Empire during his missionary journeys.

Sailing in summer

In summer in the Mediterranean, ancient mariners could sail using the sun, stars and landmarks to guide them, as the skies are clear enough to allow this. However, before the introduction of the compass, they found it very difficult to navigate in winter, with its bad storms. Fog and cloud obscured the sun and stars (see Acts 27:12).

Generally, sailing masters sailed only

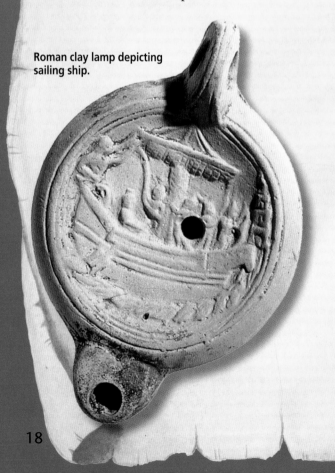

Roman clay lamp depicting sailing ship.

A fourth-century fresco of St Paul from a catacomb in Rome.

between May 27 and September 14, and at the outside from March 10 to November 10. Sailing during the late autumn and winter was only done if it was absolutely necessary – for instance to carry vital letters, to transport essential supplies or to move soldiers in a hurry.

In the Mediterranean, the wind tends to come from the north. (This is known as the prevailing wind direction.) Most ships sailing south, from Italy or Greece to Asia Minor, Syria, Egypt or Africa, could expect to make a quick and easy voyage, helped by these northerly winds. However, it was much more difficult to return against the prevailing winds, sailing north. For this reason, ships' captains or sailing masters often still chose to sail near the coast, which offered quieter waters and shelter when needed.

Storms and other dangers

However, sailing close to shore brought its own dangers. The captain found it very difficult to control his ship in a gale. Shipwrecks were common.

If there was a risk of the ship getting wrecked in a gale, the captain tried to find a port before the storm overtook his ship. For this reason, sailors valued people who could forecast stormy weather.

If a ship could not reach its final port before winter, its captain would put it into the nearest haven until sailing weather returned, even if it meant spending the whole winter in a strange port.

In addition to storms, pirates were a real danger in the Mediterranean. The Roman leader Julius Caesar (49–44 BC) finally destroyed the pirates' hideouts in Asia Minor.

Ports

One of the most ancient ports on the coast of Israel is Joppa (Jaffa), which dates back as far as the Bronze Age. King Solomon transported cedar wood from Lebanon to construct the Temple in Jerusalem via the port of Joppa (2 Chronicles 2:16).

By 700 BC, ports with sea walls began to be built around the Mediterranean, to create a place for ships to anchor safely. Gradually, quays, warehouses and defensive towers were added to create secure ports for trading.

In such ports would have been many types of small water-craft, usually powered by oars and a small sail. River and coastal boats towed larger ships and carried goods from the merchant ships to warehouses on the dockside. By 400 BC, Piraeus, the port of Athens, Greece, was surrounded by many covered warehouses that handled the goods passing through the port.

Tyre, another important port on the coast of Israel, was originally an island. In 332 BC the Greek general Alexander the Great built a causeway connecting the port to the mainland, and this eventually became a connecting strip of land.

By Roman times, much of the Mediterranean Sea and most major rivers in the region had well-equipped ports. From the time of the Roman Emperor Augustus, the eastern shores of the Mediterranean also had excellent ports, the best in Judea being at Acre (Akko), Caesarea Maritima and Jaffa.

Caesarea was the most impressive of these. It was built by Herod the Great and named after the Roman Emperor (Caesar). Engineers built a 60-metre- (200-foot-) long breakwater where vessels could moor and dock. There was also a semi-circular sea-wall that formed a kind of marina where ships could safely anchor. As many as 100 Roman war galleys could anchor at one time in the docks at Caesarea.

Paul's voyage and shipwreck

The Greek doctor, Luke, wrote a detailed account of many of the apostle Paul's adventures. In Acts chapter 27 he describes vividly Paul's voyage to Rome on his way to be tried before the Emperor.

After his third missionary journey, Paul had been arrested by Roman soldiers in the Temple precincts in Jerusalem. To protect him from Jewish enemies, he was then taken to Caesarea, where he was kept in jail for two years.

Paul was called to stand in court in turn before the Roman governor Felix and his successor Festus, as well as the Jewish King Agrippa. Eventually Paul appealed as a Roman citizen for his case to be heard before Caesar in Rome. His only "crime" was that he believed Jesus rose from the dead!

Paul was put in the charge of a Roman centurion, who took him with other prisoners on board a ship leaving for the coast of Asia Minor, as this was in the right direction. When they arrived at Myra, a port on that coast, they were fortunate to find a big grain-ship had stopped there on its way from Egypt to Rome. They transferred to this ship. During the voyage the grain-ship from Alexandria in which Paul was sailing was wrecked.

Here is Luke's account of events leading up to the shipwreck:

Paul sails for Rome

When the time came, we set sail for Italy. Paul and several other prisoners were placed in the custody of an army officer named Julius, a captain of the Imperial Regiment. And Aristarchus, a Macedonian from Thessalonica,

Smith's Bay, Malta, possible site of Paul's shipwreck.

was also with us. We left on a boat whose home port was Adramyttium [west of Troas]; it was scheduled to make several stops at ports along the coast of the province of Asia.

The next day when we docked at Sidon, Julius was very kind to Paul and let him go ashore to visit friends so they could provide for his needs. Putting out to sea from there, we encountered headwinds that made it difficult to keep the ship on course, so we sailed north of Cyprus between the island and the mainland. We passed along the coast of the provinces of Cilicia and Pamphylia, landing at Myra, in the province of Lycia. There the officer found an Egyptian ship from Alexandria that was bound for Italy, and he put us on board.

We had several days of rough sailing, and after great difficulty we finally neared Cnidus. But the wind was against us, so we sailed down to the leeward side of Crete, past the cape of Salmone. We struggled along the coast with great difficulty and finally arrived at Fair Havens, near the city of Lasea. We had lost a lot of time. The weather was becoming dangerous for long voyages by then because it was so late in the autumn, and Paul spoke to the ship's officers about it.

"Sirs," he said, "I believe there is trouble ahead if we go on – shipwreck, loss of cargo, injuries, and danger to our lives." But the officer in charge of the prisoners listened more to the ship's captain and the owner than to Paul. And since Fair Havens was an exposed harbour – a poor place to spend the winter – most of the crew wanted to go to Phoenix, farther up the coast of Crete, and spend the winter there. Phoenix was a good harbour with only a south-west and north-west exposure.

The storm at sea

When a light wind began blowing from the south, the sailors thought they could make it. So they pulled up anchor and sailed along close to shore. But the weather changed abruptly, and a wind of typhoon strength (a north-easter, they called it) caught the ship and blew it out to sea. They couldn't turn the ship into the wind, so they gave up and let it run before the gale.

We sailed behind a small island named Cauda, where with great difficulty we hoisted aboard the lifeboat that was being towed behind us. Then we banded the ship with ropes to strengthen the hull. The sailors were afraid of being driven across to the sandbars of Syrtis off the African coast, so they lowered the sea anchor and were thus driven before

The Roman forum, once the centre of the Roman Empire.

A papyrus scroll of Bible times.

the wind.

The next day, as gale winds continued to batter the ship, the crew began throwing the cargo overboard. The following day they even threw out the ship's equipment and anything else they could lay their hands on. The terrible storm raged unabated for many days, blotting out the sun and the stars, until at last all hope was gone.

No one had eaten for a long time. Finally Paul called the crew together and said, "Men, you should have listened to me in the first place and not left Fair Havens. You would have avoided all this injury and loss. But take courage! None of you will lose your lives, even though the ship will go down. For last night an angel of the God to whom I belong and whom I serve stood beside me, and he said, 'Don't be afraid, Paul, for you will surely stand trial before Caesar! What's more, God in his goodness has granted safety to everyone sailing with you.' So take courage! For I believe God. It will be just as he said. But we will be ship-wrecked on an island."

The shipwreck

About midnight on the fourteenth night of the storm, as we were being driven across the Sea of Adria, the sailors sensed land was near. They took soundings and found the water was only 120 feet deep. A little later they sounded

again and found only 90 feet. At this rate they were afraid we would soon be driven against the rocks along the shore, so they threw out four anchors from the stern and prayed for daylight. Then the sailors tried to abandon the ship; they lowered the boat as though they were going to put out anchors from the prow. But Paul said to the commanding officer and the soldiers, "You will all die unless the sailors stay aboard." So the soldiers cut the ropes and let the boat fall off.

As the darkness gave way to the early morning light, Paul begged everyone to eat. "You haven't touched food for two weeks," he said. "Please eat something now for your own good. For not a hair of your heads will perish." He took some bread, gave thanks to God before them all, and broke off a piece and ate it. Then everyone was encouraged, and all 276 of us began eating – for that is the number we had aboard. After eating, the crew

Paul's friends in Greece.

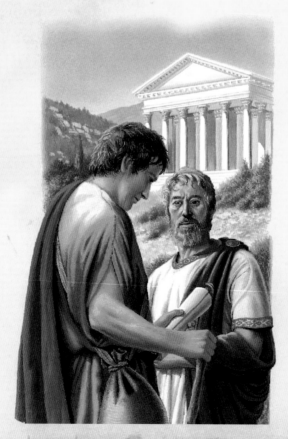

lightened the ship further by throwing the cargo of wheat overboard.

When morning dawned, they didn't recognize the coastline, but they saw a bay with a beach and wondered if they could get between the rocks and get the ship safely to shore. So they cut off the anchors and left them in the sea. Then they lowered the rudders, raised the foresail, and headed towards shore. But the ship hit a shoal and ran aground. The bow of the ship stuck fast, while the stern was repeatedly smashed by the force of the waves and began to break apart.

The soldiers wanted to kill the prisoners to make sure they didn't swim ashore and escape. But the commanding officer wanted to spare Paul, so he didn't let them carry out their plan. Then he ordered all who could swim to jump overboard first and make for land, and he told the others to try for it on planks and debris from the broken ship. So everyone escaped safely ashore!

(Acts 27, NLT)

From Luke's story, we can see how difficult it was to handle an ancient sailing ship in a gale. From Myra, at the extreme south of Asia Minor, the ship sailed west towards Cnidus, 21

Artist's impression of Luke, who wrote up Paul's experiences.

at the extreme south-west of Asia Minor. An offshore wind drove the vessel south, and the ship-master had to look for shelter beside the 224-kilometre- (140-mile-) long island of Crete (Acts 27:7). Fair Havens, where the ship sheltered, was about half-way along the coast of Crete, just east of a group of mountains.

Paul's voyage was delayed till after the Jewish fast of Yom Kippur (the Day of Atonement) at the beginning of the Jewish year, in late September/early October. Paul advised the ship's captain to spend the winter at Fair Havens (Acts 27:9). The captain, who probably also owned the ship, preferred to try to finish the voyage, instead of staying in Crete for the winter and paying big hotel bills.

A north-east wind from the highlands of Crete (Acts 27:14) drove Paul's ship south from the good port of Phoenix across 37 kilometres (23 miles) of rough sea to the island of Cauda. While the ship was sheltered by the island, the captain hauled in the ship's boat, which had been being towed behind, full of water (Acts 27:16).

South of Cauda lay Syrtis Major (the Gulf of Sydra), an area of quicksands and whirlpools. Many ancient ships sank there. Underwater archaeologists have discovered the remains of a number of these vessels. Aware of this danger, the captain of Paul's ship battled to keep her on a westerly course, and was helped when the wind veered to the east.

At this point (Acts 27:17) the crew "banded the ship with ropes to strengthen the hull". Thick cables were stored on board larger vessels to wrap around (undergird) the ship during emergencies. These cables, used to strengthen the timbers against the stresses caused by the sea and the strain from the mast, may have been passed over the deck, to form a network that could be twisted very tight.

After leaving Cauda, the sailors threw the "equipment" or "tackle" overboard. This probably consisted of the rigging and long spar from which the mainsail hung, because it was likely to become uncontrollable during a storm.

After the wreck

After the shipwreck on the island of Malta, Paul continued his voyage in a new ship to the grain-port of Puteoli on the mainland of Italy. The new vessel had the sign of Castor and Pollux (Acts 28:11). Castor and Pollux were twin brothers, mythical sons of Zeus, and the patrons of ancient sailors. They were supposed to take special care of ships caught up in storms. The stern-post of the boat probably had a carving of these twins, known in Latin as the "*Dioscuri*". Sailors seem particularly to have liked these gods, who they hoped would protect their ship.

Prison of Paul, Philippi.

Paul's end

Once he arrived in Rome, Paul was allowed to stay in his own house, with a single guard. This light imprisonment lasted two years, after which he was probably set free. He may then have journeyed to Spain to preach the gospel there.

But eventually, around AD 64-65, Paul was arrested again. He was executed in Rome for continuing to spread the Christian faith.

Paul writing from a prison cell in Rome.